World PROJECTS

By Anna Prokos

Contents

What Is an Atlas?

the Himalayas in Asia

the Amazon River in
South America

This book is an atlas – a book of maps.
In this atlas there are maps of eight regions
of the world: North America; South America;
Africa; Europe; Asia; Australia, New Zealand,
and the Pacific Islands; Antarctica and
the Arctic. There is also a map of the
United Kingdom and the Republic of Ireland.

Each map shows the countries in
a region. They show mountain ranges,
rivers and lakes. They also show some
famous landmarks. You can use the maps
in this book to find many different places
in the world.

Niagara Falls in
North America

the Sphinx in Egypt

Using an Atlas

Some tools that are used in this atlas are shown on the map on these pages. These will help you find what you are looking for.

A locator map shows where each region is found in the world.

Each country in a region is shown in a different colour. This makes it easier to tell the countries apart.

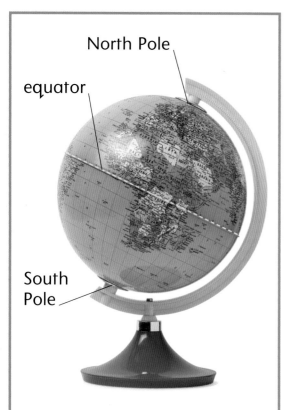

North Pole

equator

South Pole

The equator is an imaginary line around the middle of Earth. It's the same distance from the North Pole as it is from the South Pole. Usually the closer an area is to the equator, the hotter its climate. The farther an area is from the equator, the colder its climate.

Asia

Asia is home to r world's people. The highest mountain, N the world's largest l

Mars Express leaves the Baikonur Cosmodrome in Kazakhstan on a mission to Mars.

Cypru
Leba
Beir
Jerusalem
Israe

A
F
R
I
C
A

Red
Sea

The Taj Mahal is in India.

16

The equator is shown as a dotted blue line.

National boundaries in each region are shown with solid lines.

Capital cities in each region are shown with star symbols. Other major cities are shown with red dots.

Disputed boundaries are shown with dotted lines.

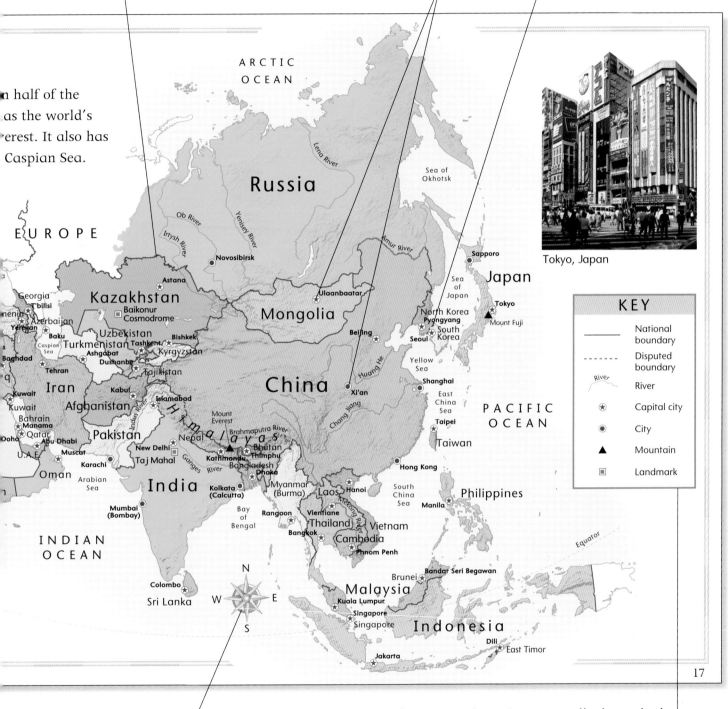

n half of the
as the world's
erest. It also has
Caspian Sea.

ARCTIC
OCEAN

Russia

Lena River

Sea of
Okhotsk

EUROPE

Ob River

Irtysh River

Yenisey River

Novosibirsk

Georgia
T'bilisi

Astana

Kazakhstan

Baikonur
Cosmodrome

Ulaanbaatar

Amur River

Sapporo

Sea
of
Japan

Japan

Tokyo, Japan

Armenia
Yerevan

Azerbaijan

Baku

Caspian
Sea

Uzbekistan

Tashkent

Bishkek

Mongolia

North Korea
Pyongyang
South
Korea

Tokyo

Mount Fuji

Turkmenistan

Ashgabat

Dushanbe

Kyrgyzstan

Beijing

Seoul

Baghdad

Tehran

Tajikistan

Yellow
Sea

Iraq

Iran

Kabul

China

Shanghai

PACIFIC
OCEAN

Kuwait

Kuwait

Afghanistan

Islamabad

Xi'an

Huang He

East
China
Sea

Bahrain
Manama

Qatar
Doha
Abu Dhabi
U.A.E.

Pakistan

Indus River

Himalayas

Mount
Everest

Nepal

Kathmandu

Brahmaputra River

Bhutan
Thimphu

Chang Jiang

Taipei

Taiwan

Muscat

Karachi

New Delhi

Taj Mahal

Ganges
River

Bangladesh
Dhaka

Hong Kong

Oman

Arabian
Sea

India

Kolkata
(Calcutta)

Myanmar
(Burma)

Laos

Hanoi

South
China
Sea

Philippines

Manila

INDIAN
OCEAN

Mumbai
(Bombay)

Bay
of
Bengal

Rangoon

Vientiane

Thailand

Mekong River

Vietnam

Bangkok

Cambodia

Phnom Penh

Colombo

Sri Lanka

N

W   E

S

Brunei

Bandar Seri Begawan

Malaysia

Kuala Lumpur

Singapore

Singapore

Indonesia

Equator

Dili
East Timor

Jakarta

KEY

——————	National boundary
- - - - - -	Disputed boundary
~River~	River
✩	Capital city
◉	City
▲	Mountain
▣	Landmark

A compass rose shows the directions on a map:
N points to North, E points to East,
S points to South and W points to West.

A key contains pictures called symbols. On a map, symbols stand for different things found in an area. The key explains what the symbols stand for.

17

The World

This map shows the different land areas on Earth.
It also shows the Earth's oceans. About three-quarters
of the Earth's surface is covered by water.

ARCT

NORTH
AMERICA

ATLANTIC
OCEAN

A

Equator

SOUTH
AMERICA

PACIFIC
OCEAN

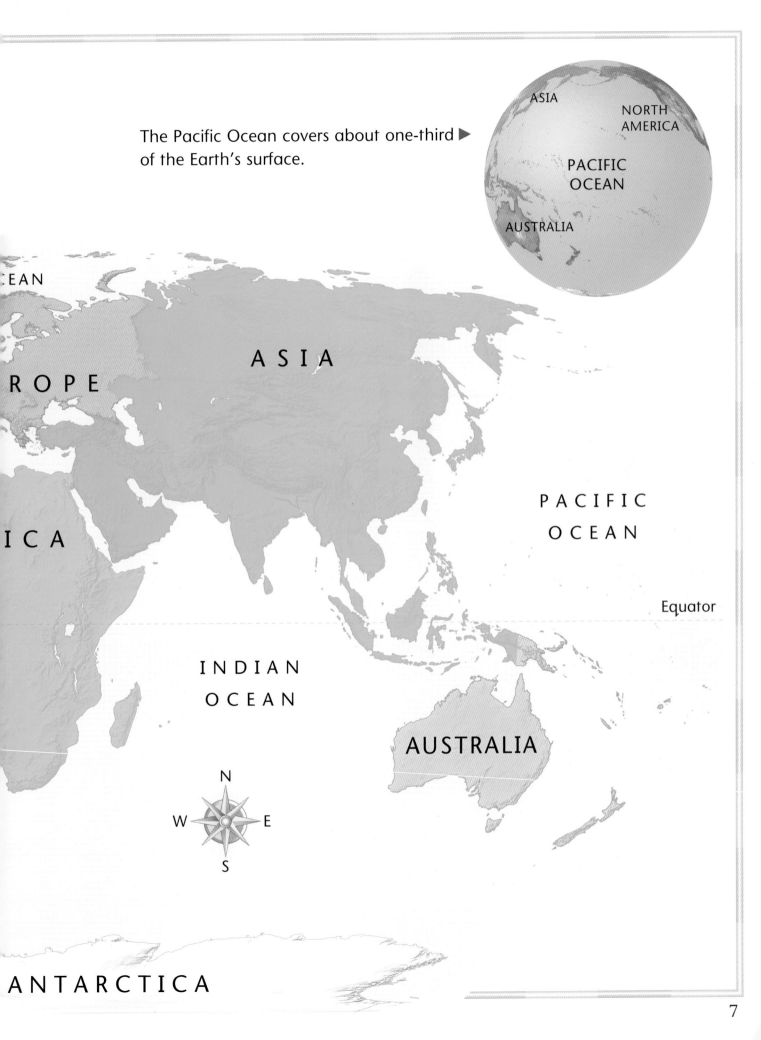

The Pacific Ocean covers about one-third ▶ of the Earth's surface.

ASIA
NORTH AMERICA
PACIFIC OCEAN
AUSTRALIA

CEAN

ROPE

ICA

ASIA

PACIFIC OCEAN

Equator

INDIAN OCEAN

AUSTRALIA

N
W · E
S

ANTARCTICA

North America

North America has nearly every type of land. Mountains, forests, deserts, jungles and tundra are all found there. The world's longest national boundary separates Canada from the United States.

The CN Tower can be seen in Toronto's skyline.

Bryce Canyon is in the southwestern United States.

ASIA

ARCTIC OCEAN

Alaska
(United States)

Mount McKinley ▲

Mackenz

Rocky Mou

PACIFIC
OCEAN

Vancouver

San Francisco

Los Angeles

Hawaii
(United States)

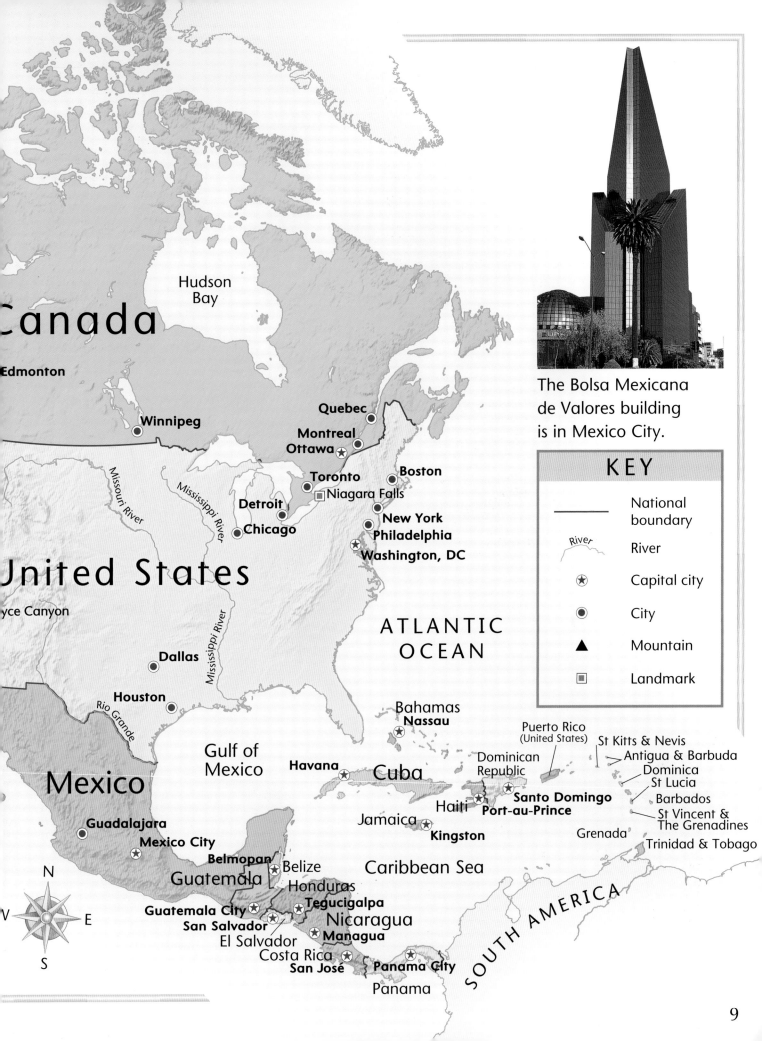

Hudson
Bay

Canada

Edmonton

Winnipeg

Missouri River

Mississippi River

Quebec

Montreal
Ottawa ★

Toronto
🔳 Niagara Falls

Detroit
Chicago

Boston

New York
Philadelphia
Washington, DC ★

United States

yce Canyon

Mississippi River

Dallas

Houston
Rio Grande

Gulf of
Mexico

Mexico

Havana ★

Guadalajara

Mexico City ★

Belmopan ★ Belize
Guatemala
Honduras

Guatemala City ★
San Salvador ★
El Salvador

Tegucigalpa ★

Nicaragua
Managua ★

Costa Rica
San José ★

Panama City ★

Panama

ATLANTIC
OCEAN

Bahamas
Nassau ★

Cuba

Jamaica ★
Kingston

Caribbean Sea

Puerto Rico
(United States)

Dominican
Republic

Santo Domingo ★
Haiti ★★
Port-au-Prince

St Kitts & Nevis
Antigua & Barbuda
Dominica
St Lucia

Barbados
St Vincent &
The Grenadines

Grenada

Trinidad & Tobago

Grenada

SOUTH AMERICA

N
W   E
S

The Bolsa Mexicana
de Valores building
is in Mexico City.

KEY

———	National boundary
River	River
★	Capital city
⦿	City
▲	Mountain
🔳	Landmark

9

South America

South America has the longest mountain range in the world. It is called the Andes. The Amazon rainforest is in South America, too.

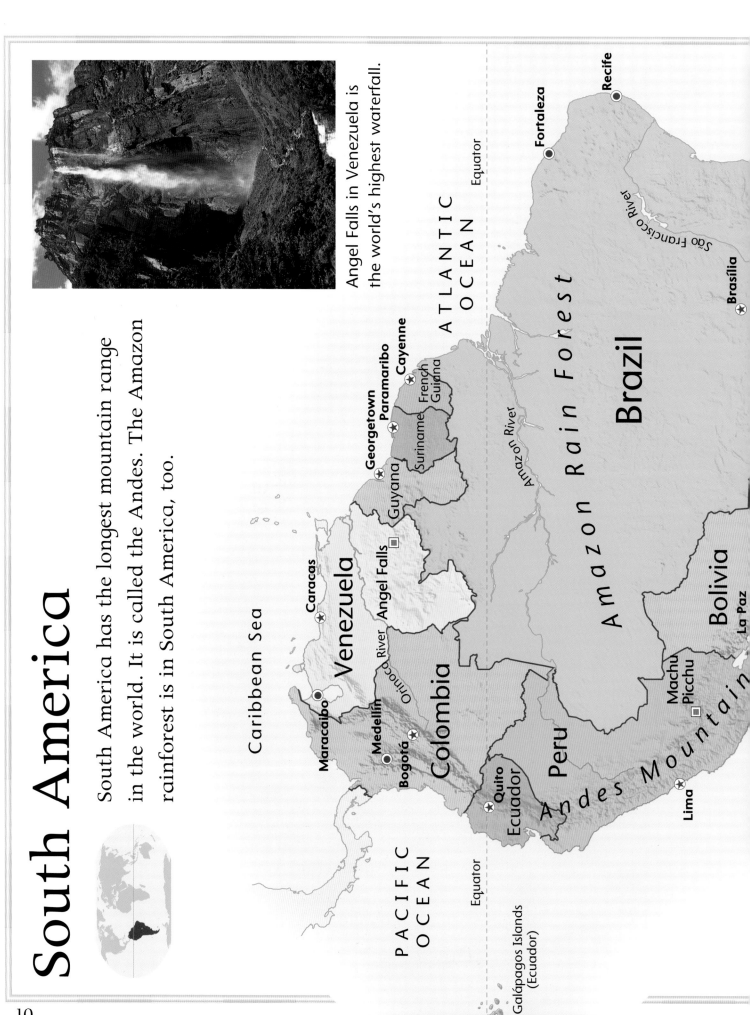

Angel Falls in Venezuela is the world's highest waterfall.

Caribbean Sea

PACIFIC OCEAN

ATLANTIC OCEAN

Equator

Galápagos Islands (Ecuador)

Maracaibo

Caracas

Venezuela

Medellín

Bogotá

Colombia

Quito

Ecuador

Peru

Lima

Machu Picchu

Bolivia

La Paz

Andes Mountain

Angel Falls

Orinoco River

Georgetown

Guyana

Paramaribo

Suriname

Cayenne

French Guiana

Amazon River

Amazon Rain Forest

Brazil

Brasília

São Francisco River

Fortaleza

Recife

Equator

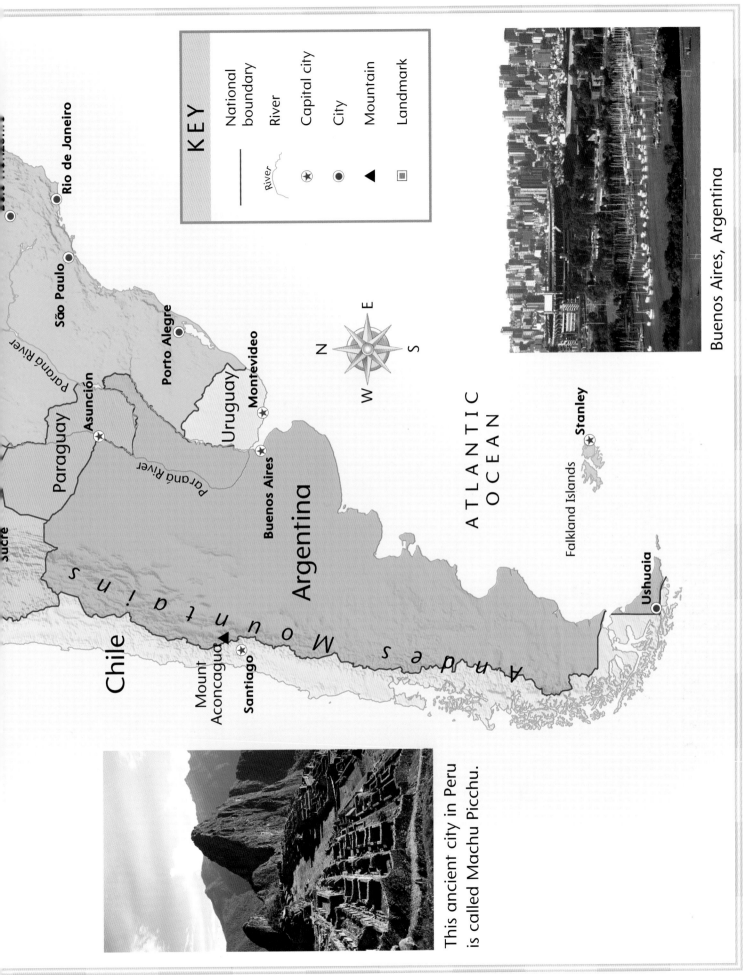

KEY

National boundary

~~~ River

★ Capital city

◉ City

▲ Mountain

▫ Landmark

Rio de Janeiro

São Paulo

Porto Alegre

Paraná River

Asunción

Paraguay

Paraná River

Uruguay

Montevideo

Sucre

Chile

Andes Mountains

Mount Aconcagua

Santiago

Argentina

Buenos Aires

N
W · E
S

ATLANTIC OCEAN

Falkland Islands

Stanley

Ushuaia

Buenos Aires, Argentina

This ancient city in Peru is called Machu Picchu.

Africa

Africa has the largest desert in the world. It is called the Sahara. The world's longest river is in Africa, too. It is called the Nile.

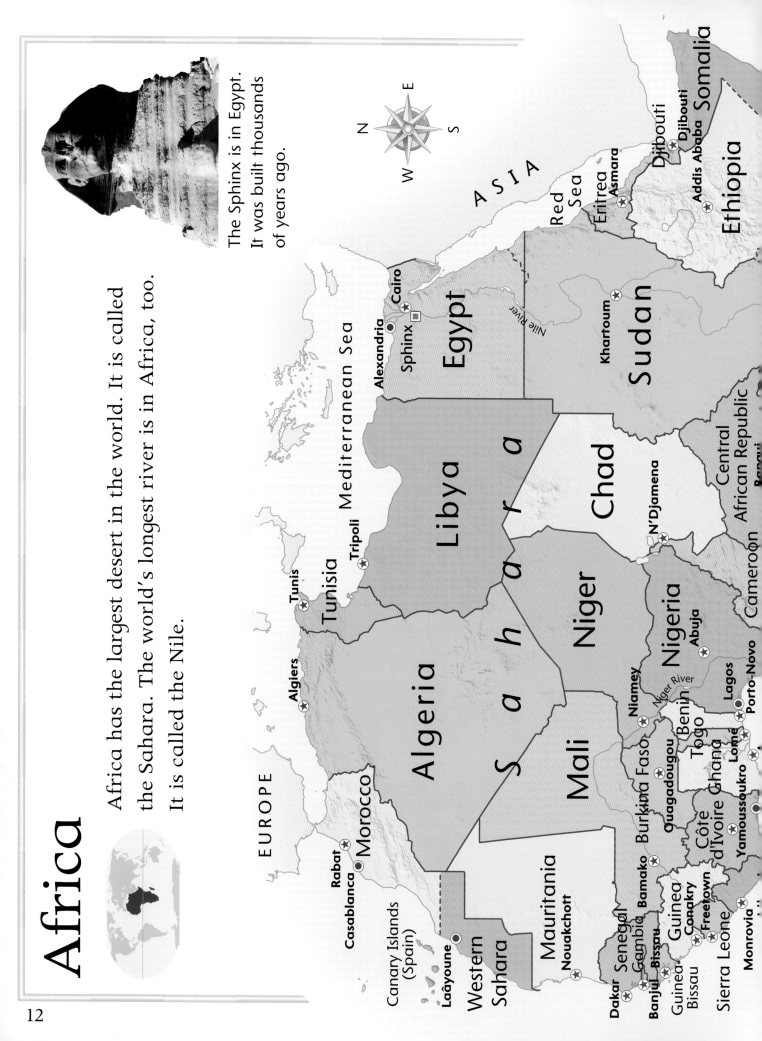

The Sphinx is in Egypt. It was built thousands of years ago.

N E S W

ASIA

EUROPE

Mediterranean Sea

Red Sea

Canary Islands (Spain)

Laâyoune

Western Sahara

Morocco
Rabat
Casablanca

Algiers

Tunis
Tunisia
Tripoli

Algeria

Libya

Egypt
Alexandria
Cairo
Sphinx

Nile River

Khartoum

Sudan

Eritrea
Asmara

Djibouti
Djibouti
Addis Ababa

Ethiopia

Somalia

Mauritania
Nouakchott

Mali
Bamako

Niger
Niamey

Chad
N'Djamena

Central African Republic
Bangui

Sahara

Dakar
Senegal
Gambia
Banjul
Guinea-Bissau
Bissau
Guinea
Conakry
Sierra Leone
Freetown
Monrovia

Burkina Faso
Ouagadougou

Niger River

Benin
Togo
Lomé
Côte d'Ivoire
Yamoussoukro
Ghana
Accra

Nigeria
Abuja
Lagos
Porto-Novo

Cameroon

12

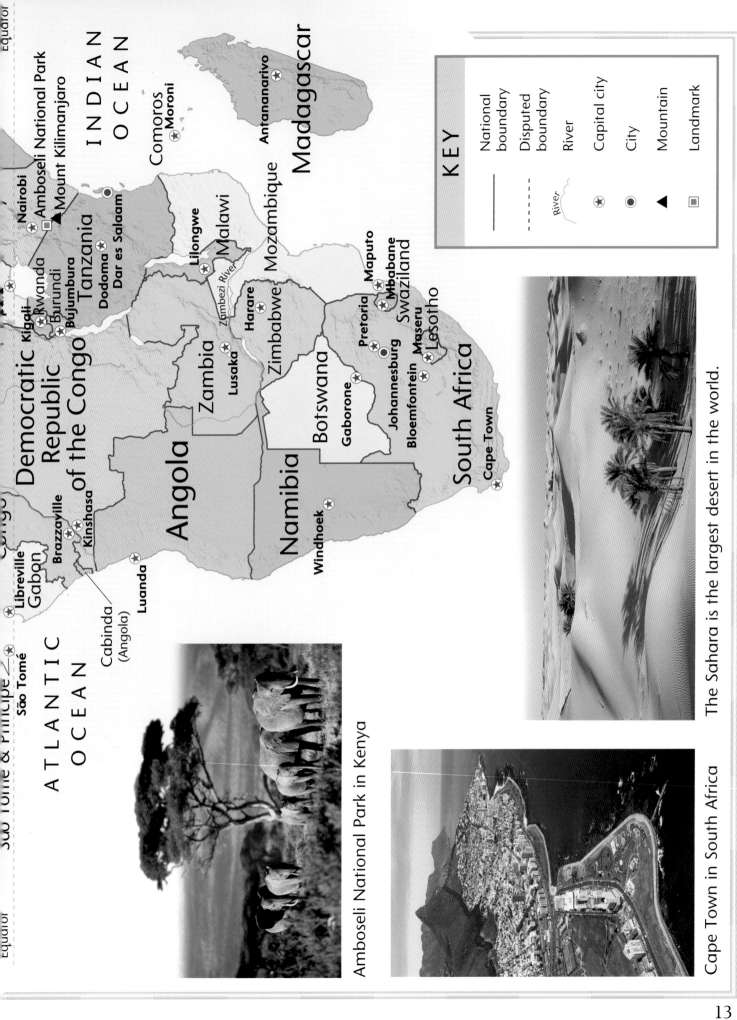

Equator

São Tomé & Príncipe

ATLANTIC OCEAN

São Tomé

Libreville
Gabon

Brazzaville
Kinshasa

Cabinda
(Angola)

Luanda

Congo

Democratic
Republic
of the Congo

Angola

Namibia

Windhoek

Kigali
Rwanda
Burundi
Bujumbura
Kigali

Nairobi
Amboseli National Park
Mount Kilimanjaro

Tanzania

Dodoma
Dar es Salaam

Zambia

Lusaka

Zimbabwe

Harare

Zambezi River

Lilongwe
Malawi

Mozambique

Botswana

Gaborone

Pretoria

Johannesburg
Bloemfontein

South Africa

Cape Town

Maputo

Mbabane
Swaziland

Maseru
Lesotho

INDIAN OCEAN

Comoros
Moroni

Antananarivo

Madagascar

KEY

National
boundary

Disputed
boundary

River

Capital city

City

Mountain

Landmark

Amboseli National Park in Kenya

Cape Town in South Africa

The Sahara is the largest desert in the world.

Europe

Europe has the Alps mountain range which starts in France and ends in Slovenia. There are more than forty countries in Europe.

Big Ben is in London.

The Alps mountain range spreads through many European countries.

Reykjavík
Iceland

N
W E
S

Norwegian Sea

Norway
Oslo
Swed
Stockholm

North Sea

Edinburgh
Belfast
Ireland
Dublin
United Kingdom
Birmingham
Big Ben London

Denmark
Copenhagen

Baltic

Netherlands
Amsterdam
Hamburg
Berlin
The Hague
Brussels
Belgium
Luxembourg
Germany
Pola

Rhine River

Prague
Czech Repu
Slova

Paris
Luxembourg

ATLANTIC OCEAN

France

Danube River
Munich
Vienna
Brati
Liechtenstein
Bern
Switzerland
Austria
Budapest
Hung

Mont Blanc ▲ A l p s
Milan Ljubljana Slovenia
Zagreb
San Marino
Croatia Belg
Bosnia
Herzegov

Portugal
Andorra
Lisbon
Madrid
Spain
Monaco
Barcelona

Italy
Rome
Vatican City

Sarajevo

Tiran
Alb

Mediterranean Sea

AFRICA

Malta
Valletta

14

Finland

Helsinki ★

St. Petersburg ⊙

Tallinn ★
stonia

Riga ★
Latvia

ithuania

Vilnius ★

Minsk ★

iningrad
Russia)
rsaw

Belarus

Russia

Moscow ★

Volga River

Don River

ASIA

Dnieper River

Kiev ★

Ukraine

Moldova

Chisinau ★

Romania

Bucharest ★

Black Sea

a &
tenegro

Bulgaria

Sofia ★

Istanbul ⊙

onje
cedonia

Turkey

reece

Athens ★
□ Parthenon

Moscow is the largest
city in Russia.

The Parthenon is in Athens, Greece.

KEY

——	National boundary
River	River
★	Capital city
⊙	City
▲	Mountain
▣	Landmark

Asia

Asia has the highest mountain in the world. It is called Mount Everest. The world's largest lake is in Asia, too. It is called the Caspian Sea.

Mars Express leaves the Baikonur Cosmodrome in Kazakhstan on a mission to Mars.

The Taj Mahal is in India.

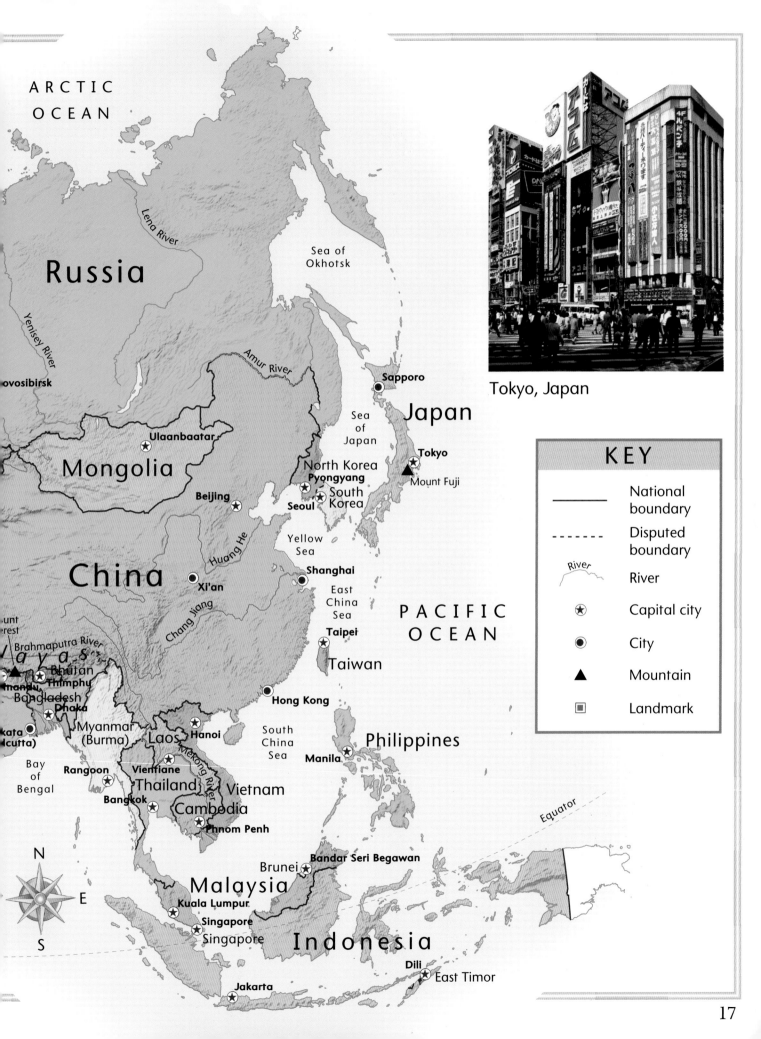

ARCTIC
OCEAN

Russia

Lena River

Yenisey River

ovosibirsk

Sea of
Okhotsk

Sapporo

Japan

Sea
of
Japan

Tokyo

Mount Fuji

Amur River

Ulaanbaatar

Mongolia

North Korea
Pyongyang

Beijing

South
Korea

Seoul

China

Xi'an

Huang He

Yellow
Sea

Shanghai

East
China
Sea

PACIFIC
OCEAN

Chang Jiang

Taipei

Taiwan

unt
rest

Brahmaputra River

ayas

Bhutan
Thimphu

mandu

Bangladesh

Dhaka

Hong Kong

South
China
Sea

kata
lcutta

Myanmar
(Burma)

Laos

Hanoi

Philippines

Mekong River

Manila

Bay
of
Bengal

Rangoon

Vientiane

Thailand

Vietnam

Bangkok

Cambodia

Phnom Penh

N

Bandar Seri Begawan

Brunei

Malaysia

Equator

E

Kuala Lumpur

S

Singapore
Singapore

Indonesia

Dili
East Timor

Jakarta

Tokyo, Japan

KEY

———	National boundary
- - - -	Disputed boundary
River	River
⭐	Capital city
◉	City
▲	Mountain
▣	Landmark

17

Australia, New Zealand and the Pacific Islands

This region is made up of Australia, New Zealand, Papua New Guinea and the Pacific Islands. Australia has the largest coral reef in the world. It is called the Great Barrier Reef.

Equator

INDIAN OCEAN

Darwin

Broome

Australia

Uluru □ **Alice Springs**

Perth

Adelaide

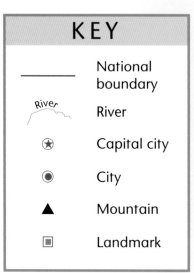

Sydney is the largest city in Australia.

KEY

———	National boundary
River	River
⊛	Capital city
⊙	City
▲	Mountain
▣	Landmark

N
W   E
S

The emu is found only in Australia.

Uluru is in Australia's central desert region. It is a monolith, or large block of stone.

18

Papua
New Guinea

Lae

Solomon
Islands

Port Moresby

Honiara

The Great Barrier Reef is the
largest coral reef in the world.

PACIFIC
OCEAN

Vanuatu

Port-Vila

Fiji

Suva

Great Barrier Reef

Cairns

Nouméa

New
Caledonia
(France)

Brisbane

Darling River

traditional thatched houses in Fiji

Murray River

Sydney

Canberra

Auckland

Melbourne

New
Zealand

Wellington

Hobart

Aoraki

Aoraki in New Zealand

Christchurch

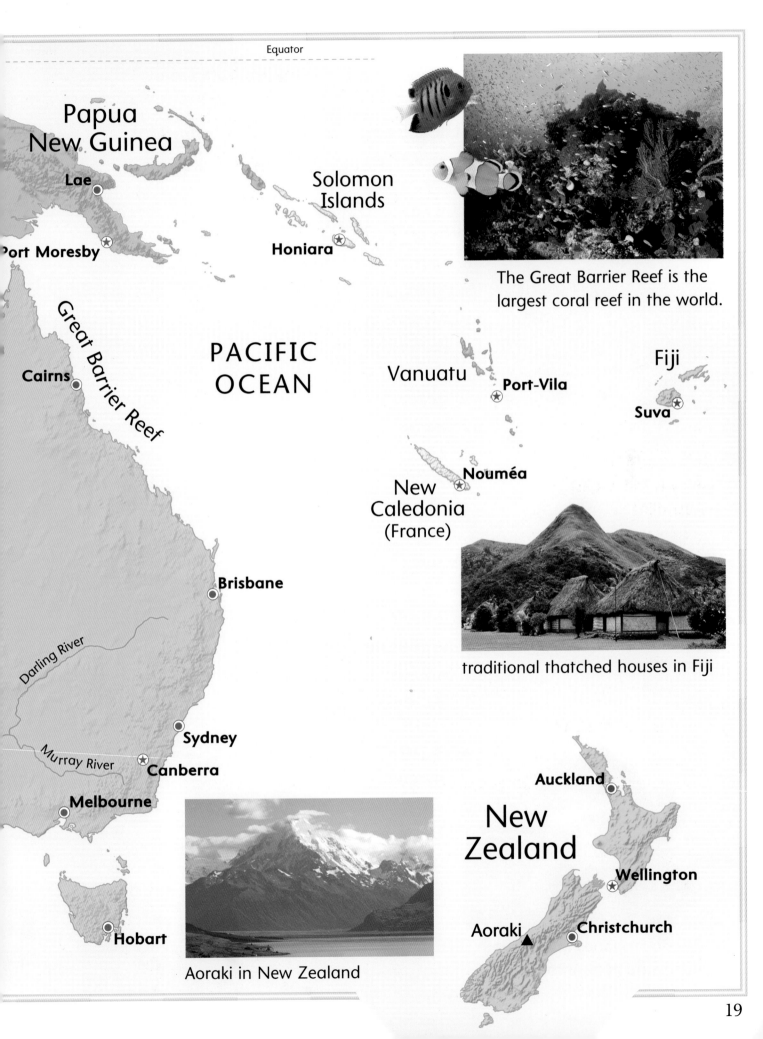

Antarctica

Antarctica is the coldest, driest and windiest place on Earth. Scientists from many countries work in Antarctica.

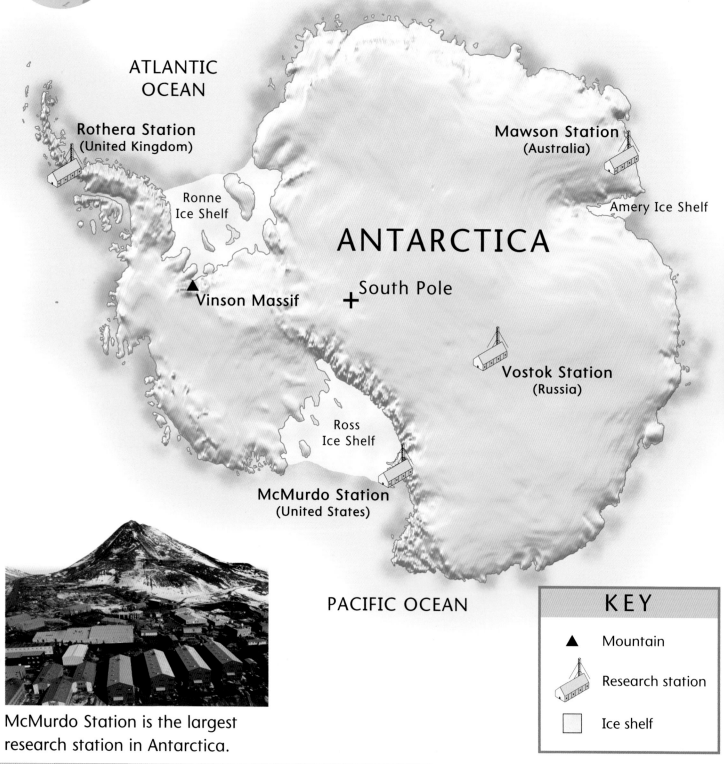

ATLANTIC OCEAN

Rothera Station
(United Kingdom)

Mawson Station
(Australia)

Ronne
Ice Shelf

Amery Ice Shelf

ANTARCTICA

▲ **Vinson Massif**

＋ South Pole

Vostok Station
(Russia)

Ross
Ice Shelf

McMurdo Station
(United States)

PACIFIC OCEAN

KEY

▲ Mountain

⛺ Research station

☐ Ice shelf

McMurdo Station is the largest
research station in Antarctica.

The Arctic

The Arctic Ocean and the northern parts of North America, Europe and Asia make up the Arctic region.

The polar bear lives in the Arctic.

KEY

★ Capital

◉ Town

▢ Ice cap

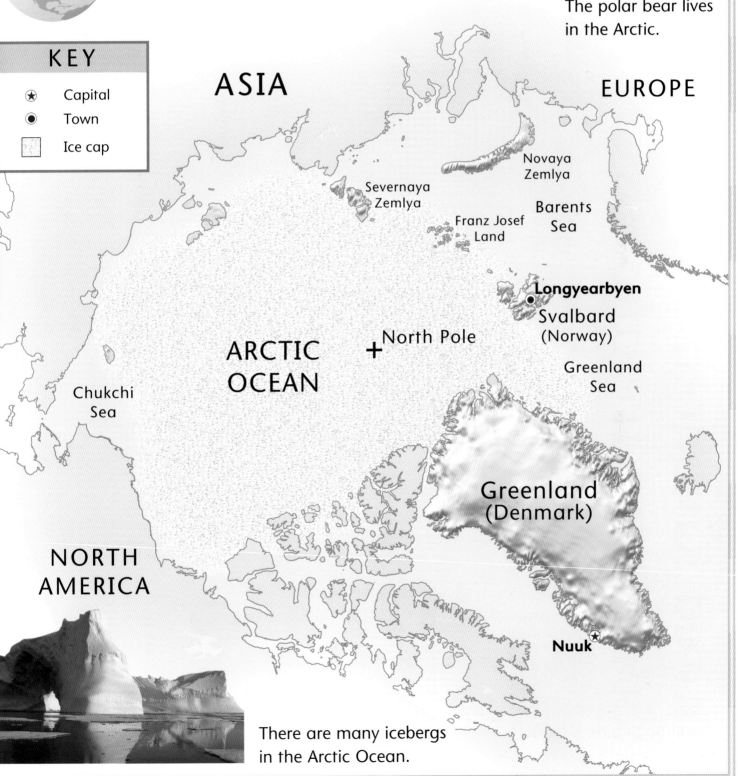

ASIA

EUROPE

Novaya Zemlya

Severnaya Zemlya

Franz Josef Land

Barents Sea

Longyearbyen
Svalbard (Norway)

Greenland Sea

ARCTIC OCEAN

+ North Pole

Chukchi Sea

Greenland (Denmark)

NORTH AMERICA

Nuuk

There are many icebergs in the Arctic Ocean.

United Kingdom and Republic of Ireland

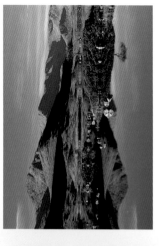

The Scottish Highlands have mountains, glens and lochs

The United Kingdom is made up of England, Scotland, Northern Ireland and Wales. The Republic of Ireland is an independent country.

Shetland Islands

Orkney Islands

Aberdeen ◉

Dundee ◉

Inverness ◉

Scotland

▲ Ben Nevis

Edinburgh ★

Glasgow ◉

Western Isles

The Angel of the North in Gateshead is more than 20 metres high.

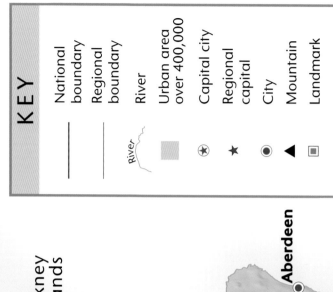

North Sea

Giant's Causeway in Northern Ireland has amazing rock columns.

ATLANTIC OCEAN

Sunderland

Angel of the North

Northern
Ireland

Bangor

Belfast

United Kingdom

Scafell Pike

Isle of Man

Irish Sea

Dublin

Anglesey

Snowdon ▲

Kingston upon Hull

York

Leeds

Bradford

Manchester

Preston

Liverpool

Chester

Stoke-on-Trent

Sheffield

River Trent

England

Derby

Nottingham

Leicester

Wolverhampton

Birmingham

Coventry

Norwich

Peterborough

Cambridge

London

Canterbury

Brighton

Portsmouth

Isle of Wight

Southampton

Stonehenge

River Thames

Oxford

Gloucester

River Severn

Bristol

Wales

Newport

Cardiff

Swansea

Exeter

Plymouth

English Channel

Channel Islands

N
E
S
W

Republic
of Ireland

Galway

Limerick

Waterford

Cork

The Millennium Stadium
in Cardiff was built for the
Rugby World Cup in 1999.

Stonehenge is a famous site of ancient
stones begun around 3,500 years ago.

23

Index